Tulips

Victoria Blakemore

For Silvana, Laura, Karen, and Leta, without whom I wouldn't know the first thing about floral design ✻

Copyright info/picture credits

Cover, karandaev/AdobeStock; Page 3, MabelAmber/Pixabay; Page 5, Couleur/Pixabay; Page 7, Storyblocks; Page 9, davidraynisley/Pixabay; Page 11, hcast/AdobeStock; Page 13, Olesia Sarycheva/AdobeStock; Page 15, Marta Jonina/AdobeStock; Page 17, black_horse/Pixabay; Page 19, manfredrichter/Pixabay; Page 21, stux/Pixabay; Page 23; Storyblocks; Page 25, 3dman_eu/Pixabay; Page 27, Nikolai Sorokin/AdobeStock; Page 29, Anna Parzychowska/AdobeStock; Page 31, karandaev/AdobeStock; Page 33, Storyblocks

Table of Contents

What Are Tulips?

Tulips are flowers. They are members of the lily family. Other members of the lily family include aloe, bear grass, bellwort, and lilies.

Tulips come in many different colors and shades. They can be red, purple, orange, yellow, white, pink, and even black.

Some tulips can be a mix of

different colors.

3

History

Tulips were originally wild flowers that grew in parts of Central Asia. They were **cultivated** in Turkey over one thousand years ago.

They were very popular in Turkey for many years. At one time, it was a crime to sell tulips outside of the capital city.

Their name comes from a Turkish word for turban. This is because of the tall, rounded shape of their petals.

Tulip Mania

Tulips were first brought to the Netherlands in the 1590's. They quickly became very popular.

As they became more popular, they became more expensive. They were once the most expensive flowers. They were even used as money in parts of Europe.

Tulips were most popular between the years of 1634 and 1637. This time is known as "tulip mania." At the time, a tulip could cost more than a house!

Life Cycle

The tulip life cycle has four main stages. First, a bulb is planted in soil. With enough water and nutrients, it will grow into a sprout.

The sprout grows a stem. The stem grows leaves and a flower. The seedpod is inside of the flower. This is where the seeds that become bulbs are stored.

Each part of the tulip has an important job to help the tulip grow and survive.

Bulbs

The bulb is the part of the tulip that is planted in the soil. It is larger than most plant seeds.

Bulbs are planted several inches under the soil. When it gets cool enough, the bulb will begin to grow roots down into the soil.

Bulbs that are healthy are firm. They are not dry or mushy. The larger bulbs usually **produce** larger blooms.

Roots

The roots grow from the tulip bulb. They grow downward into the soil and help to **anchor** the plant. They keep it in place as it grows.

The roots are also responsible for taking in **nutrients** from the soil. These **nutrients** help the tulip to grow and stay healthy.

The roots also provide the tulip

with water from the soil. A single

bulb may have many long roots.

Stems

The stem grows upwards from the bulb. The stems are long, thick, and hollow. They grow towards the sun, so they may lean in one direction.

The stem helps to transport water and nutrients from the roots to the other parts of the plant.

Leaves

The leaves grow from the bulb like the stem. Tulip leaves are long, thin, and have a pointed tip at the end.

Tulip leaves have an important job. They make energy from sunlight in a process called **photosynthesis**.

Tulip leaves can look like very

thick grass if there are no

blooms.

Flowers

Tulip flowers are brightly colored and usually only last for about a week. Their bright colors help to **attract** pollinators such as bees.

Tulip flowers are made up of three petals and three **sepals**. They look alike so it can be hard to tell them apart.

Inside the flower are six stamen.

The stamen have the pollen that

pollinators collect.

Pollination

Tulips can be **pollinated** in several ways. They are able to transfer pollen to the **stigma** on their own.

The wind, animals, and people can also help to pollinate tulips and spread seeds. Once a tulip is **pollinated**, it is able to make seeds.

Pollinators such as bees collect pollen from tulips. When they fly to different flowers, they spread the pollen.

Where are Tulips Grown?

Tulips need colder climates to grow. The colder temperatures cause the bulbs to start sending out roots.

Bulbs should be planted in the fall. That way, their roots can start to grow before it gets too cold. Tulips bloom for up to a week in the spring.

Blooming tulips are often thought of as a sign that spring has arrived.

Tulips are grown in many different places. There are tulip fields in countries such as the United States, Turkey, Italy, Germany, and Russia.

The Netherlands is often called the tulip capital of the world. They grow and **export** more tulips than any other country.

The Netherlands **exports** over

three billion tulips to other

countries each year.

Tulip Festivals

Some places have tulip festivals that celebrate the blooming of the tulips every spring.

Tulip festivals include tours of tulip fields, tulips for sale, and contests where you can enter tulips you have grown. People can also learn how to grow and take care of tulips.

In places such as Amsterdam, a parade of flowers is held each spring. Colorful floats are decorated with only springs flowers such as tulips.

Eating Tulips

Most tulip petals are **edible**, which means that they can be eaten. They can be used to replace onions in many recipes.

Tulip petals were often eaten by Dutch people who didn't have enough food during the second world war. They were added to bread, soup, and salads.

Symbolism

Flowers and colors are often used to **symbolize** different ideas and feelings. Tulips themselves are often thought to **symbolize** love.

Red flowers, such as tulips and roses are usually used to represent love.

Purple tulips are used to

represent royalty.

White tulips can have several meanings. One of them is forgiveness. They can also be used to **symbolize** respect.

Pink tulips can be used to send a message of caring or good wishes. They are often given to a friend or family member.

Yellow and orange tulips can

both stand for happiness,

energy, and **enthusiasm**.

Glossary

Anchor: to keep stable or in place

Attract: to cause to come near

Cultivated: when a plant is planted on purpose and helped to grow

Edible: able to be eaten

Enthusiasm: a strong interest in something

Export: to send to another country to sell

Nutrient: something that helps people, plants, or animals to grow

Photosynthesis: the process a plant uses to make sunlight into energy

Pollinated: when pollen has been transferred to a flower, allowing it to make seeds

Produce: to make

Sepal: the parts of the flower that support the petals

Stigma: the part of a flower where pollen is put to help it make seeds

Symbolize: to represent or stand for something

About the Author

Victoria Blakemore is a first grade

teacher in Southwest Florida with a

passion for reading.

You can visit her at

www.elementaryexplorers.com

Also in This Series

ray Wolves	Sloths	Flamingos	Camels	Koalas	Honey Bees	Pandas
Pangolins	White-Tailed Deer	Orcas	Giraffes	Corn	Meerkats	Echidnas
Walruses	Raccoons	Bald Eagles	Apples	Arctic Foxes	Red Pandas	Cassowaries
Tigers	Ladybugs	Moose	Beluga Whales	Leopards	Elephants	Jellyfish
Binturongs	Lions	Dolphins	Reindeer	Hammerhead Sharks	Hippos	Pumpkins
Peafowl	Chameleons	Florida Panthers	Aye-Ayes	Black Bears	Cheetahs	Manatees
Gingerbread	Polar Bears	Hot Chocolate	Orangutans	Coyotes	Marshmallows	Strawberries

Also in This Series

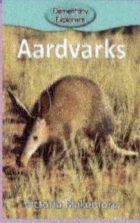

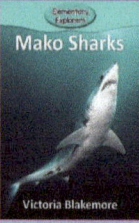

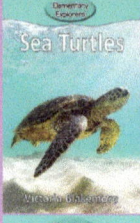

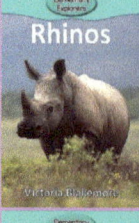

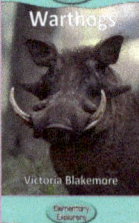

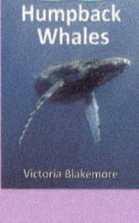

Aardvarks	Mako Sharks	Alligators	Frogs	Hedgehogs	Brown Bears	Bongos
Sea Turtles	Quokkas	Muskrats	Zebras	Red Foxes	Ring-Tailed Lemurs	Platypuses
Anteaters	Kangaroos	Rhinos	Jaguars	Wombats	Capybaras	Gorillas
Cats	Skunks	Butterflies	Dingoes	Snow Leopards	African Wild Dogs	Penguins
Whale Sharks	Wolverines	Warthogs	Caracals	Badgers	Seals	Hummingbird
Pikas	Humpback Whales	Pumas	Lemonade	Llamas	Tulips	

Victoria Blakemore

www.ingramcontent.com/pod-product-compliance
Lightning Source LLC
Chambersburg PA
CBHW051254020426
42333CB00025B/3205